The Sit 'N' Do Nothing

Hamster Series

Humans **A**ll **M**ake **S**ome **T**ime **E**xploring **R**elationships

Written By Wendy Proteau

The Sit N Do Nothing Series

Covers designed by: Wendy Proteau

The Sit N Do Nothing Series

The Single Man Hamster

Volume Two

Why a Hamster, we all have a hamster. It is that continual engine that keeps spinning the wheel in our minds. We think every moment of every day. Choices, twists, turns, preferences, decisions, experiences, work, home, business…every moment of every day thinking constantly! What do you want out of life? How do you feel about life in general? What are your goals and dreams?

I'm betting your life is busy, doing what needs to be done. You have hobbies, work, goals, schedules…so I'm thinking you rarely take time just to look at it all. You're here now so let's have some fun with this.

You are an accumulation of every moment up until now. You've lived, laughed, helped, cared and probably touched more lives than you thought. Do you realize how many people you affect in life? Do you recall the memories and share them with others?

These aren't hard questions and they cover a variety of topics. Some are things men think about and some are what women have always wondered about. We've been on this earth together for thousands of years and we still don't understand the other gender. Men are men-women are women. That's the beauty of it all, that mysterious draw to one another.

You have several people in your life, best friends (both male and female), parents, step-parents, brothers, sisters, co-workers, even people you see every day through routine. Do you talk about all the things you've done, admit to the mistakes, glory in the successes or share past memories?

With the world moving so fast we are ever in search of what we want in life. Would you recognize what that was if it were right in front of you or are you so busy that you've missed opportunities along the way?

Let's just stop for a moment and reflect on it all. There is just one rule to this book-

"GOTTA BE HONEST!"

So grab a pencil, a drink, and kick your feet up on the coffee table. Let's begin….

Male Hamster Basics

Little known facts about ________________ and what I think
(First name please)

Today's date is:_________________

So let's start with the basics of who you are on paper

Last name________________________________

I live in _________________________________

Born ______day _________ month _______year

Born in_______________________________

Time I was born was at_______________________

Raised in__________________________________

Other places I've lived over the years:

____

____

____

____

Education level is _________________________

I went to the following schools-name and year please:

____

____

____

I work as a________________________________

I have been at my current job ________years

I have worked in my trade _____years

This book was given to me by____________________________

In 5 words I would describe who I am as

1________________________________

2________________________________

3________________________________

4________________________________

5________________________________

In 5 words I would describe the person who gave me this book as

1_______________________________

2_______________________________

3_______________________________

4_______________________________

5_______________________________

See, not so hard is it…..
SO LET'S START HAVING SOME FUN

THE SINGLE MAN HAMSTER
Volume Two

1-Well here you are, so let's see what you're all about, shall we? What traits do you think you possess? Check off only what you would say defines you. Now you can't be all of these things so only the ones that apply to how you see yourself. You're going to mark them on a scale from 0-10 (0 = not me at all up to 10 which means yep, that is totally me)

Honest	_____	Charming	_____
Independent	_____	Funny	_____
Laid back	_____	Open book	_____
Stubborn	_____	Strait forward	_____
Strong values	_____	Hard-working	_____
Passionate	_____	Sensual	_____
Loyal	_____	Strong work ethic	_____
Shy	_____	Mysterious	_____
Strong willed	_____	Intelligent	_____
Smart ass	_____	Coy	_____
Lazy	_____	Creative	_____
Artistic	_____	Introvert	_____
Extrovert	_____	Family oriented	_____
Animal lover	_____	Quick witted	_____
Sarcastic	_____	Soft hearted	_____
Loner	_____	Flirtatious	_____
Hard to understand	_____	Heart on your sleeve	_____

2-See, that wasn't so hard. Now these, you're either one or the other, some you may relate to both…but which one describes you more on each line:

Book smart	______	Street smart	_______
Mr. Popular	______	Bit of a loner	_______
Mechanically inclined	______	I don't own tools	_______
Dreamer	______	Realist	_______
Man of his word	______	I tend to fib	_______
Aggressive	______	Passive	_______
Know what you want	______	You'll figure it out later	_______
Romantic at heart	______	Not into all that stuff	_______

3-What do you think women would say about your looks? Using the list below, you are going to number each one in order from 1-14 of what you think women would say are your best features. Number 1 would be your most attractive feature and number 14 would be your least attractive feature (by the time you're done you should have a number on each)

Hair	_____	Biceps	_____
Legs	_____	Eyes	_____
Teeth	_____	Butt	_____
Smile	_____	Arms	_____
Abs	_____	Chest	_____
Cheekbones	_____	Jaw line	_____
Feet	_____	Calves	_____

4-What one thing would you like to change about yourself from the above list if you could?

Change____

Why____

5-Now think back over your life and use two words to describe yourself for each of the ages below and be sure to include what you felt was your best physical feature at that age. If you haven't reached all the ages listed, think about the future and what you hope will be

Age	Two words that defined you		Best feature
15	__________	__________	__________
20	__________	__________	__________
30	__________	__________	__________
40	__________	__________	__________
50	__________	__________	__________
60	__________	__________	__________
70	__________	__________	__________
80	__________	__________	__________
90	__________	__________	__________

6- Since we're looking back on your life, think about all the fun things you've gone through and answer each of these questions.

Who was your first crush on ____________________

Did you ever go out with them ________

Who first had a crush on you ____________________

Did you like that they did ________

Who was your first date with ________________________________

How old were you __________

First girl you kissed was ________________________________

Who was your first real girlfriend ________________________________

How long did it last __________

Which babysitter did you have a crush on ____________________________

First real wow kiss was from _________________________________

7-Since we're covering your early years, let's think about more of the things you did way back when. There was so much to learn to get to where you are now. Here are some more firsts to reflect on:

First toy you ever had was ____________________________________

First sport you loved playing ____________________________________

First car you drove was a ____________________________________

First car you owned was a ____________________________________

First accident-car was a ____________________________________

First best friend was ____________________________________

First big mistake and you got caught by your parents was when

____

First drink you had you were how old______

First girl you had sex with was _____________________________________

Where were you when it happened _____________________________________

First game you every played ______________________________

First hobby you took up ______________________________

First vacation was to ______________________________

First job you had was ______________________________

8-Now let's think on the overall picture of things. Let's go with the bests so far in life. No saying you won't have better, just think up until now.

Best vehicle you ever had was a ______________________________

Best date you ever had was with ______________________________

Best friend you ever had ______________________________

Best teacher was ______________________________

Best day was when you ____

Best kiss was from ______________________________

Best sex was with ______________________________

Best laugh was with ______________________________

Best pet you ever had was ______________________________

Best purchase you ever made was ______________________________

Best toy you have now ______________________________

9-So with the bests, comes the worsts. Yep, can't have one without the other. So might as well write those all down.

Worst vehicle you ever owned ______________________________

Worst date was with ______________________________

Worst teacher was ______________________________

Worst day was when you______________________________

Worst kiss was from ______________________________

Worst sex was with ______________________________

Worst friend turned out to be ______________________________

Worst pet you ever had ______________________________

Worst toy you ever had ______________________________

Worst job you ever had ______________________________

10-Whew, it's hard to think back on all those things. Some make you chuckle…what we're ya thinking back then? While we're reminiscing, if you could run into one of your ex-partners/girlfriends from the past, who would you most like to see now face to face and have a conversation with?

Who: ______________________________

Why:

____

____

11- And if you could see one of them, but they not see you…kinda a fly on the wall scenario just to see how their life is, which one would it be? Remember they wouldn't know you're checking up on them.

Who: ______________________________

Why:

____

____

12-How about we find out more about you; which of these would describe who you are. You don't have to own it, just pick the one which you can relate to more. Now you can only choose one on each line, so check off which one describes you more.

a- Truck____ Sports car ____ Motorcycle ____ Off-road _____Beater_____

b- Fine dining ____ Fast food ____ Home cooking ____ Frozen dinner_____

c- Wine ____ Beer ____Hard stuff_____ Soda____ Water____

d- TV ____ Music ____ Reading ____ Sports_______

e- Action ____ Mystery _____Drama _____Romance ____ Sci-fi ____Thriller ____

f- Email ____ Phone ____ Text ____ In person_____

g- Quiet ____Talkative ____Joker ____Tough guy____

13-Now we all love movies, they take us away to places we never thought of. If you could actually live out any one movie, which movie would you like to experience for real? Think about it…

Movie: ____

Which character would you like to be: _______________________

Why:____

____

14-Speaking on the movie topic, which kind of scene would you like to jump into just once? You know, try it out just for the fun of it. There are probably a few, so number them in order of preference. (1 being I'd definitely do that one first etc…) You can add one option:

Star wars flying scene __________

Wild-west shoot out __________

Bar room brawl __________

Food fight ___________

Love scene ___________

Dare devil jumps ___________

Action hero ___________

Porno ___________

Hit man ___________

Martial arts ___________

Police/detective ___________

War scene ___________

Other____

15-Now I know you're supposed to not show them, but some have fears in life, things we just don't like. It could be heights, spiders, while some even have multiple fears…do you have any? I am Afraid of:

___________________ ________________ _________________ ______________

16-This is all about your favorites in life. We all have them and I'm betting people in your life just don't know them all. So here we go…what are/is your favorite:

Color ___________________

Food____

Fast food____

Drink____

Saying____

Song____

Band____

Song to dance to____ (even when alone)

Candy bar___________________________

Song to sing to____

Place to be____

Sport________________________________

Past time____

Way to kill time____

Friend to spend time with________________________

Animal_________________________

Wild animal___________________________

17-Do you cook? You must on some level, you have to eat. Let's ask this simple question and you can only be one of these five options. You consider yourself:

_______A chef->I can make anything

_______A cook-> love it but stick to what I know

_______BBQ God->as long as it is on a grill I can do it

_______Boxed->if it comes in a package with instructions I'm ok

_______Take out king->I just can't eat my own cooking

This will apply to most of you. Even if you can't cook well, try to pick out the following:

What is your best dish ____

What would your friends say it is ____

What would you cook for a date ____

What would you serve for a hot date ____

18-Ok let's probe that head of yours. Being single, what are the first things that attract you to a partner/woman? Now these are all things you can see from a distance because you don't know them, but you're watching from across the room or see someone online. Rate these in order of importance 1= what I notice first, 10 being last thing I check out.

Eyes	_______	Hair	_______
Smile	_______	Body shape	_______
Confidence level	_______	Way she dresses	_______
Behavior	_______	Chest	_______
Legs	_______	Butt	_______

19-So you spotted them across that room and you're curious…so what's next Sherlock? What are your methods-what would you do?

If online would you send a message ____yes ____no
If yes, what would you type?

____

If in person would you

Send a drink	____ yes ____ no
Try to get them to notice you by smiling	____ yes _____ no
Get the waitress to talk to to them for you	____ yes _____ no
Would you just not do anything	____ yes _____ no

Or would you use the direct approach where you walk up and you would say:

____

Do you use some line to try to break the ice, if so, what is your best line

____

What is first question you'd ask:

____

I guess there are many ways of approaching. Some have tried and true methods and some wing it!

20-Some people are afraid to approach. I guess fear of rejection is on both sides these days. Sometimes it's the friends razzing you afterwards. Do you ever wonder how many you missed out on from being afraid to try? Let's find out. In your mind, the worst thing that could happen if you approach and they're not interested is...

____

How many do you figure you missed out on by not approaching ______

21-Well I admit it's not so easy to approach a perfect stranger, so they now have the world of computer date sites. There are many to choose from, even specialty ones, from size to wealth and preferences. How you feel about all these sites?

Would you try one _______yes ______no

How many have you tried________

If yes, did you meet anyone interesting _______yes ______no

How many dates didn't work out _______

How many were off the wall totally _______

How many ended up as friends _______

How many relationships of yours started from the computer ______

How many would you have liked to get to know more but never did ________

Worst off the wall date was named: ______________________________

Describe what happened:

____

____

22-Now being the world of technology, you look at a picture/read a profile and chat online for a bit. Really, it opens you up to more possibilities in the world, not just dating locally. Friends can be made all over the world. If you've tried a site, how do you handle getting to know someone you've sparked an interest in?

How long do you like to talk online first ________ days/months

Do you want to meet in person right away ______yes _____no

Do you prefer talking on the phone first _______yes ______no

How would you like to meet them: ____in a group setting ____ one on one

Do you meet on neutral ground ______yes ____no

Do you go to their area _____yes _____no

23-Ahhhh…the dating world, it's not an easy thing. I wonder how you feel about this progressive society we are living in? How do you feel about each of the following:

Women making first contact:

____

Women asking you out:

____

Women paying for the date:

____

Women kissing you first:

____

Women wanting to pay their own way:

____

24-Well some people are more comfortable when things are done a certain way when it comes to the dating world. Answer each of the following when it comes to how things usually go in your date life. For a first date your preferences would then be:

Prefer to be the one asking _______% of the time

Prefer to make the plans ________% of the time

Prefer if she makes the plans _______% of the time

You like to just meet at the neutral place _______% of the time

Prefer to pick her up _________% of the time

Likes if she pays _________% of the time

You prefer to pay ________% of the time

You prefer to make the first physical move ______% of the time

25-Now we've been on this earth together for thousands of years and we still don't understand each other. What are the top 5 things that women do that just drive you nuts? You just don't understand why they do these things:

1-____

2-____

3-____

4-____

5-____

26-Now put the shoe on the other foot. What five things do you do that just ticks women off or they stand their saying what the?

1-____

2-____

3-____

4-____

5-____

27-Now that you've thought of the worst, what are the top five things women do that just make it all worth going through:

1______________________________________

2______________________________________

3______________________________________

4______________________________________

5______________________________________

28-If you're single now, you must have a list of things that you value and look for in a partner. We all need that physical attraction, but what specifics make us want to hold on to someone? Besides being attracted physically, check off what you think is important to you in finding that perfect woman. These are only a few things I could think of, some may apply…some of no importance to you, so don't check them all.

Feisty/fiery	_____	Strong work ethic	_____
Stubborn	_____	Loyalty	_____
Independent	_____	Hygiene	_____
Soft hearted	_____	Well-dressed	_____
Integrity	_____	Confident	_____
Passionate	_____	Stable	_____
Good hearted	_____	Loves kids	_____
Intelligent	_____	Loves animals	_____
Easy going	_____	Active	_____
Understanding	_____	Athletic	_____
Humorous	_____	Driven	_____
Strong willed	_____	Family Values	_____
Caring	_____	Religious	_____
Financially stable	_____	Honesty	_____
Morals	_____	Expressive	_____
Background	_____	Sensual	_____
Quiet	_____	Shy	_____
Outspoken	_____	Homebody	_____
Successful	_____	Education	_____

Now that you've figured out what you truly value, go back and number them in priority. Number 1 is the most important thing to you and so on.

29-Made you think on that one. I'm surprised the book wasn't thrown across the room along with a few choice swear words. Okay, so this should be an easy one for you. What are the absolute deal breakers for you in a relationship? You just will not tolerate:

1-____

2-____

3-____

4-____

5-____

30-Let's change the subject for a bit. We've all done some crazy things in our life that we look back and shake our head saying…why did I? The craziest thing for you would be when:

____

____

Now along with that goes with the most fun thing we did and we still smirk when we think about it, so that would be when you:

____

____

31-If you were given the opportunity to do things and it was all set up for you, paid for etc…would you: (Some you may have done already)

Bungee jump ____yes____ no
Skydive ____yes____ no
African safari ____yes____ no
Mountain Climb ____yes____ no
Motor cross race ____yes____ no
Cliff dive ____yes____ no

Drive a race car ____yes____ no
Bronc riding ____yes____ no
Be a stuntman ____yes____ no

Now thinking along those lines, many things are becoming more and more possible everyday with technology. So if it ever became available to you, would you?

Take a trip into space _____yes____ no
Dive to the bottom of the ocean in a submarine _____yes____ no
Take a ride in an air force jet _____yes____ no

32-Thinking back, we all had a dream when we were growing up. We all thought we'd grow up to be a fireman, policeman, marine biologist, etc…

What did you want to be when you were young?______________________________

Did you go to University/College to get a degree _____yes ____no

Did you stick with it _____yes _____no

What did you take ____

Did you take a break from school figuring you'd work for a while then go back to pursue an education ______yes _______no

What line of work are you in now ____

Do you like what you do ______yes _____no

If you could have any job right now, anything at all, what would you like to be doing:

____

What do you think your friends would say you'd be best at

____

33-Looking back over all the relationships you've had, if you could re-live a time in your life with a particular partner…like go back in time to one moment…

A-If you could live it exactly the same all over, exactly as it happened and not change a single thing:
How old would you be: ________ Who was it with: ____________________________

What was it: ____

____

B-Now, if you could go back and change one moment, like go back and change something you did or said:

How old would you be: __________ Who was it with:___________________________

What would you change____

____

C-If you could go back and change your path in life, perhaps decided to remain with someone or never have been with someone:

How old would you be: _________ Who was it with:____________________________

What would you liked to have done____

____

34-These days everything seems a lot tougher. I sometimes wonder about life and how it would be to experience a total other century. How would it be if I were born in the fifties? Well my friends tease saying I'd probably still have the tough life-(nice friends I have)

So let's ask you, if you could go back and live for one year in a different time, what era would you like to be part of?

Era: __________________________

What would you have been:____

Why would you like to see that era?

____

What do you think your friends would say you'd be back then

____

35-Now on that same thinking, if time travel were possible and you could glimpse at only one time period, what would you like to see and why? Think hard it could be way in the future or way back.

Times of__________________________________

What would you like to see most ____

36-Those are fun to think of, aren't they? Bet you never thought of stuff like that or maybe you have and just never had to write em down. Would be interesting to see what your friends would say to those. Speaking of friends….

A-Who's your best male friend right now? ______________________________________

How long you known him? _____________

Where'd ya meet?____

What do you like most about him?____

What is his best physical feature?____

What do you dislike most about him?____

B-Who's your best female friend right now: _____________________________________

How long you known her? ______________

Where'd ya meet?____

What do you like most about her?____

What is her best physical feature?____

What do you dislike most about her?____

How many friends do you have all together roughly? _________

Who do you always count on when ya need something? ___________________________

37-Thinking about your best friends, what do you think they'd say is the best thing about you?

Male friend would say:____

Female friend would say:____

38-Now I asked some single males to help me out here with thoughts that flit through a man's mind when they meet someone of interest. I wonder how many of you are on the same line of thinking. I put the scenario that she was hooked up to a lie detector and she didn't know who the questions were coming from or that she was hooked up for that matter-YIKES!
What 10 questions would most men ask? Below are all the suggested one's, but you can only choose 10 in total. Now they might not think like you, so I left space for you to add 3 of your own…Remember 10 only-(including yours!) Number the one's that you'd ask in order of importance, #1 being the very first question you'd want an answer to.

_____are you high maintenance

_____are you looking to get married

_____are you wanting children

_____do you drink heavily

_____how many partners you had

_____do you like sports

_____are you gonna try and change me

_____ever thought of cheating or cheated

_____do you really enjoy sex

_____are you honest

_____how many men have you had sex with

_____are you independent

_____are you really established

_____have you ever had an STD

_____would you ever consider a three way

_____are you overly needy

_____ any drug addictions

_____are you a couch potato in disguise

_____was money ever a factor in your other relationships

_____are you still hooked on a former boyfriend or lover

_____-____

_____-____

_____-____

Add three of your own (if needed). Remember only 10 in total!)

39-Throughout your life you've probably met a bunch of people and I'm sure you have a few fond memories of them all, but over your lifespan the best friends have usually been:

Men ______ or Women ______

40-Famous people: If you could meet them face to face, it could even be people you grew up either listening to their music or watching them on the big screen…who would you really like to meet? (past or present, living or gone)

TV star:___________________________

Movie star_________________________

Sports star_________________________

Band_____________________________

Singer____________________________

Race car driver_____________________

Author____________________________

Photographer______________________

Artist_____________________________

Any others__________________________

41- A friend or family member may have gotten this for you to keep ya busy and see how you think. They make the world go round, what would you do without them? So think about the person who handed you this book-If you could plan an outing with them-anything at all, maybe go fishing for a weekend, go to a movie, go riding-whatever you chose, what would it be? (Probably after this book, a long walk on a short pier!)

____

If you bought this book for yourself, if you could take one friend anywhere for an outing this weekend, what would you plan and with whom?

____

42-Lets find out more about how you live, shall we? People have a certain way of keeping their home. Now you'd only be one of these options, so would you say you're:

Neat person ______(everything where it belongs most of the time)

Messy person ______(can never find what I'm looking for)

Retentive ______(oh my don't move that or I'll have a fit)

Organized chaos ______(I know where everything is just don't move the piles)

There's no hope ______(I give up as long as I find my bed at night)

Tidy ______(I do a regular cleaning once a week)

Organized ______(can drop in anytime, its company friendly)

43-Let's find out about how you keep your appearance. This is on a regular basis when you're just hanging out at home relaxing by yourself. Put a percentage in how you spend most of the time when at home.

Can find me in sweat clothes always ________%

I wear jeans/t-shirt around the house ________%

I prefer to wear dress pants/nice shirt ________%

I don't like clothes so I wear as little as possible ________%

I just grab whatever is clean ________%

Shorts and a muscle shirt ________%

In the mornings do you follow the same routine even if you're hanging around the house? Number these in order that you do them, starting with #1:

Brush hair	______	Brush teeth	______
Shower	______	Shave	______
Get dressed right away	______	Drink Coffee	______
Smoke (if applicable)	______	Eat Breakfast	______

Do you always have a plan for the day _____yes _____no

Like to sit and figure it all out _____yes _____no

Wait for the phone to ring before you plan _____yes _____no

You shower/bath ____ times per week

Brush your teeth ____ times per day

44-Routines, I suppose we all have them and some even have the getting ready to go out routine. When you're planning a night out, how much fussing do ya do? Let's say you have a first date:

How long does it take you to get ready ________________

How many times do you change clothes _______times.

Do you take extra care with your hair _____yes _____no

Do you always shave _____ yes _____no

Do you ever ask a friend about what your wearing _____yes _____no

Do you use cologne ______yes ______no

Do you wash your vehicle ______yes ______no

Do you plan the whole date out ______yes ______no

45-Now, you're all ready to go…first date, (yikes!) and on the drive there to meet her do you:

Ever want to cancel at last minute ______yes ______no

Have you ______yes ______no

Do you always call if you can't make it ______yes ______no

Do you get nervous ______yes ______no

Do you worry about your appearance ______yes ______no

Do you ever get tongue tied ______yes ______no

Do you play out the evening in your head as you drive ______yes ______no

Do you think about the end of the night ______yes ______no

Do you think about the cost of the night ______yes ______no

How much do you like to spend on a first date on average $ ________________

46-First dates for women can be nerve wracking. The thrill, anticipation, excitement and we always wonder what the men are thinking. We would like to know what things you look for or notice about your date. How important are the following: On a scale from 1-10 (1-being, yep I care about and really like that, 10-being nope don't even notice)…how do you rate these when assessing the lady on a first date?

Dressed provocatively ______ Dressed conservatively ______

Casual clothes ______ Eye contact ______

Amount she smiles ______ Easy conversation ______

Talks about work	______	Talks about ex's	______
Asks you questions	______	Shyness	______
Fun level of date	______	Gestures by touching	______
Laughter/humor	______	Serious conversation	______
Amount she drinks	______	Amount she eats	______
Flirting	______	Amount she talks	______

47-Some people know right away whether they are attracted or not. How long does it take you to decide whether you want a second date with her?

I can tell within the first ______ minutes/seconds, if I'll see her again.

I can tell within the first ______ minutes/seconds, if I want to have sex with her

I can tell within the first ______ minutes/seconds, if I see this as a long term possibility

48-The rules have changed in dating over the years. While some still follow traditional ways taking their time, others have a fast track style and don't want to waste time before getting close. At the end of the night, you're driving your date home and you really like this woman and can see a future, so what do you prefer to happen when you walk her to the door? For each, give your opinion:

She gives a simple peck on the cheek-You would interpret that as

____

A gentle kiss that lingers-You think that means

____

A full passionate kiss tongue and all

____

Invites you in for a nightcap just to talk more

____

Her hand slides through your hair or squeezes your butt while kissing

____

She invites you in for the night (ok jump in both feet right off the bat)-

____

Wonder if any of the above make you feel differently about her? In these changing times do you judge a woman by how forward or open she is?

____yes ____no

In your own words after a perfect date with the woman you want to have a relationship with, your ideal woman would:

____

____

49-Do you have a usual pattern for dating? What do you normally like to plan for each of the following, where do you take them?

First date______________________________

Second date____________________________

Third date______________________________

Fourth date_____________________________

When do you start wanting to be exclusive: ________weeks/months/years

50-Enough on the dating stuff. Being single you enjoy a variety of things, life isn't always about women…you're a busy guy! What do you do with your free time when you're at home?

Favorite thing to do ____

Thing you end up doing most often ___________________________________

Do you play organized sports if so what ______________________________

How often do you play ___________/ week/month

What hobbies do you have ____

How often do you enjoy it _________/week/month

What's your favorite weekend thing to do

____

What's your favorite thing to do weekday evening thing to do

____

What do you wish you had more time to do

____

Do you have any projects you started and can't find time to get back to

____

51-Profound moments…we all have them! Moment's when we learn going through life's trials and tests. Sometimes they are the things that just make us stop and see everything differently. What is the one thing you learned from all your trying times up until now?

____

52-Ever wonder about other people you see in life? At times it seems others got it so easy and have it all figured out. Or at least that's what we think when we look at them. Are you envious of anyone in your life? Do you wish your life were more like someone else's? Whether it's because they are more talented, stronger, educated, wealthier…

Do you have friend envy? ______ yes _____no.

You may only envy one person or there may be more…so we'll only give you two to fill in here;

Who is it ______________________

Why ____

Who is it ______________________

Why ____

I guess if we view others as having things better, you just know there's a whole bunch out there that are much worse off than we are.

53-Then there's those people you just shake your head at. You see them every day on the drive to work, at work or just out in public. The ones who just seem to not get it at all! Those who drive crazy disregarding everyone or idiots who walk into busy traffic….it makes ya nuts at times. What's the one thing that irks you the most when you see it:

____

54-Shopping-now there's a topic for men! We all have to do it whether its groceries or the project places for buying wood for that deck or a new tool, so let's ask:

Favorite place to shop ____

Favorite thing to shop for ____

Are you a patient shopper ______yes ______ no

Will you go from store to store for the best deal _______yes ________no

Do you just run in and pick up what you need _______yes ________no

Do you like to browse around _______yes _______no

What do you hate shopping for ____

Do you like shopping with a woman _______yes _______no

Who is your favorite person to shop with ________________________________

Who do you hate shopping with the most ________________________________

Are you an informed shopper and check all the stats _______yes _______no

55-If you had extra money right now, let's say an extra $10,000 and the bills are all paid, so it's free money and you could buy anything you wanted…think about that for a minute, is there one big-ticket item or many? What would you buy?

__________________ __________________ __________________

__________________ __________________ __________________

56-Since we're talking about money, for some it is the biggest worry in the world and it never seems we have enough of it! In making our way in this world, we do what we can to make our lives what we wish. How do you feel about your financial situation right now? (now you can only be one of these options)

Doing ok	_______	I'm just making it	_______
I'm comfortable	_______	Need a second income	_______
I don't worry about it	_______	Geez I need the lotto to fix this	_______
I stress over it	_______	I'm rich, no money issues	_______

57-The stress of life with work, bills, debt, problems…is there never an end? A friend once said: 'life is not about happiness, but about those moments that make you happy.' He says we're not supposed to wake up every morning happy, but go through the motions and do what we have to. He's a bit different, but it's what he believes. So let's ask:

You go to bed every night after a hard day and when you wake in the morning, fill in each of the following lines with a percentage on each line. Only complete the ones that apply to you…but they must total 100 percent all together.

How do you wake up on average?

Feeling positive ________%

Feeling negative ________%

Just go through the motions ________%

Look forward to the day ________%

Dread leaving the bed ________%

I smile every morning ________%

TOTALS: 100 % (make sure it adds up)

Thinking about that subject, what four things make you content in your life right now, it could be the car you drive, family, the night out last week…whatever:

1-____

2-____

3-____

4-____

58-We all took classes in school that we just don't use every day, whether history, chemistry, geometry etc… If you could have taken a few course's back in school to help you out in everyday life (these are not real courses, but things you wish learned more about at a younger age) what do you wish there would have been a few classes on? It could be plumbing, mechanics, electrical, or even understanding others. For me is how not to be ripped off by mechanics course!

____

____

59-You've thought a lot about where you are in life, so looking forward over the next ten years, what things do you hope to accomplish or change? Top three would be:

1-____

2-____

3-____

60-Back to the sexy stuff! The saying is every 8 seconds you think about sex-so we're going to keep asking about it all. In your everyday life you see lots of women I'm sure, at work, friends or just people you see repeatedly. Let's see if you're holding back any thoughts: (no names so it's safe)

Do you have women who flirt with you constantly: ________yes ______ no

You flirt: _____always ____only when ya mean it ______not at all

Is there one in particular you fantasize about: ________yes ______no

Do you want to date her-do you feel a spark: ________yes ________no

Why haven't you asked them out

______scared _______ they're married ______working on it

61-Now those thoughts tend to dive into the sexual, that is what the experts say so let's see what you think:

Sex crosses your mind ________times a day

If you could you would like to have sex _____times a week/month

You consider yourself as having:

_______high sex drive

_______average sex drive

_______below average

_______you've given up

_______using the purple pill

_______don't even think about it

Your next partner must be willing to have sex at least: _______times per week

We all wish for the perfect sexual partner, so what would that be to you? A virgin who knows nothing and has much learning or someone a little more adventure seeking? Now you can only pick one. You would enjoy your new partner to be someone who is:

_______experimental

_______traditional

_______exhibitionist

_______shy

_______experienced

_______somewhat experienced

_______virgin

_______willing to try new things

Now if you're struggling with this question, I guess you may want a few options here. Perhaps I was a little unrealistic by limiting you to picking only one. Use two of your own words to describe what you hope for in your next partner:

______________________________and______________________________

62-Let's see how you feel about the following… you are usually attracted to what kind of body type. You may find a few here, so number them in order of preference with #1 being your first choice (You find them just so sexy):

_______extremely thin (model type)

_______thin

_______average

_______chunky

_______has a few extra pounds

_______pear shaped

_______chesty

_______voluptuous

_______big beautiful women

_______taller than you

_______shorter than you

_______no preference, it's the mind that attracts you

If I missed your type just add it ____

63-In all those men's magazines they always show picture perfect air-brushed women. Now we've all seen those pictures of famous people caught without the make-up and touch ups and we're kind of shocked they don't walk around looking perfect all the time. You like:

_______women who wear make-up _______don't wear make-up

_______a little is ok _______gothic (all dark_

64-We hear jokes about women who just don't look that great in the morning. I'm sure you've heard men talking about the one that he'd rather chew his arm off than wake her. (They all look better at closing time) So gotta ask:

Has that happened to you _____yes _____no

How many times so far _________

Describe the worst one the next morning

____

____

65-Now that you've finished laughing at that one, what do you just find just so sexy about a woman first thing in the morning? It could be the way they're wrapped up next to you or their messy hair:

____

66-When do you like having sex the most? Notice I didn't give you an anytime option, so you gotta choose when you just feel you're at your best…And only choose 1!

_____mornings _____afternoons

_____just home from work _____evenings

_____late nights

67-So let's find out what you've experienced so far:

Strangest place you ever had sex was:____

Most risqué place you've ever had sex:____

Favorite position is________________________________

Most uncomfortable place was:____

Most romantic place was: ____

Hot oils ______yes ______no ______want to

Toys ______yes ______no _______want to

S&M ______yes ______no _______want to

Role playing ______yes ______no _______want to

Being tied up ______yes ______no _______want to

Tied someone up ______yes ______no _______want to

Public Sex ______yes ______no _______want to

Dominatrix ______yes ______no _______want to

Multiple partner ______yes ______no _______want to

If you could find a perfect partner for you and she was open to fulfilling each of the following, but only doing so once, what would you choose:

You would like to have sex just once (where)_________________________________

You would like her to try just once____

68-Fantasies, we all like to think about things, yet we don't talk about them really that often. So here it is straight up: If you only got to live out one fantasy it would be:

____

____

69-Now we've talked about different areas of attraction, so let's say you're back at your place after a night out and things are definitely moving to the bedroom. Yep, it's your first time with this woman. What crosses a man's mind? It could be many things I suppose. Put the following in order of importance to you. (#1-being what you notice first) Remember, this is the first time with her so initial thoughts that pass through your mind:

____The look in her eyes

____The way she kisses

____The way she tastes

____Her vocal reactions

____Way her body responds

____Emotional connection

____Takes control somewhat

____Feel of her skin

____The way she looks naked

____Her sensuality

____Her touch

____Her experience level

____Positions she likes

____Lets you lead

Did I miss any in that list, is there one thing you just are captivated with during sex:

____

Connecting on an intimate level is very important. Sometimes it's there and sometimes not. What are two things that you just don't like a woman doing in the bedroom?

____

____

70-Erogenous zones…those little places that just make us go-WOW! Everyone has something different, from a caress up the back, bite on the shoulder, to a tongue on the neck. What are the two things a woman can do that just makes you crazy?

____

____

71-Now of course not all work on everyone some we just don't like at all, no matter how many other people tell us it's great. What works for one, may not work for another, so what are three things you just don't like sexually?

____

____

____

72-Some things just happen by accident, while some people are into them. It's too late when ya realize yikes, I'm marked! So let's see how you feel about these:

Hickeys _______yes _______no

Scratch marks _______yes _______no

Bruise's _______yes _______no

Bite marks _______yes _______no

73-Speaking of marks and such, I wonder if you mind any of the following or maybe you're really into the look of them on women.

A few Tattoo's _______yes _____no Major tattoo's _______yes _____no

Pierced nose _______yes _____no Pierced brow _______yes _____no

Pierced belly button _______yes _____no Pierced nipples _______yes _____no

Pierced tongue _______yes _____no Pierced lips _______yes _____no

74-Since we're talking about what you like and don't like, do you prefer a woman to dress a certain way? Let's see what styles you find more attractive. Now, we all have different types of clothes for all different occasions-(can't clean house in a gown). Put these in order of what you find most sexually appealing. (#1-what you think is the sexiest) You don't have to like them all, only number the ones that just make you tingle when you see it.

____sweats ____sun dress

____jeans/t-shirt ____shorts/muscle shirt

____short skirt ____knee length skirt

____fancy gown ____sweater

____white blouse ____dress pants

____suits-professional look ____dresses

____leather/biker wear ____bikini

____swimsuit ____strapless dress

____bathrobe ____wearing your shirt

Now the sexy stuff! For some it doesn't matter (its coming off anyhow) for others it's a turn on, so what do you like?

____Matching bra and undies ____Merry widow

____See-through lingerie ____Bustier

____Vinyl wear ____Fishnet stockings

____Nylons black stripe ____Corsets

____Satin sleepwear ____Animal print lingerie

____Leather-dominatrix style ____Lace

75-So we asked how you felt about women having markings in question 73, now it's your turn. You may even have multiples, so straight up, what do you have on your body?

Any tattoo's _______yes _______no _______want one

If yes –how many _______________

Where is it ____

What is it/are they?

____

____

Any piercings _______yes _____no ______want one

If yes how many __________

Where is it/are they

____

76-You have a certain way of dressing I'm sure, everyone has their own style, but have you ever wanted to try out a new style, even if it's for one night and you could do it with no one knowing?

If you could, would you wear any of the following, if given the opportunity to go out one day, to an appropriate function?

Suit _______yes _______no

Tuxedo _______yes _______no

Cowboy style _______yes _______no

Drag _______yes _______no

Costume ball _______yes _______no

What costume would you like to wear _______________________________

Biker gear (chaps n all)______yes _______no

Uniform _______yes _______no

What kind of uniform would you look sharp in ______________________________

Speedo _______yes _______no

Thong and bow tie _______ yes_______ no
(Chippendale dancer)

77- Sports-now there's a topic! What are your favorites?

To go to a live game (top 3)

__________________ __________________ __________________

To watch on TV (top 3)

__________________ __________________ __________________

To play (top 3)

__________________ __________________ __________________

You have season tickets for ___________, ___________, _________

Do you like to watch/attend with friends _____yes _____no

You prefer to watch them at: ______home _____ a friend's house _____at a sports bar

Best game you every saw was:

Team: ____

Year: ___________ You were with____

Why was it the best

____

____

Best game you ever played you were _______/years old

The team you were on was the ____

The sport was __________________________

Why was it the best

____

____

78-Competitive sports whether it's a group of friends, work or league play, do you:

Participate in one ______ yes _____ no _____not into sports

Do you do so on a regular basis ______yes _______no

Who is your favorite team mate ____

79-Well if you are not into competitive stuff, do you have a fitness routine? Let's just see how you feel about the following:

Do you work out _____yes _____no ______what's that

I work out at least ________times a week/month/year

I don't have a routine really, but I do work out _____yes _____no

At this very moment, I could do at least

______sit ups

______push ups

______pull ups

______jumping jacks

______bench press (in lbs)

I could jog/run for at least _______miles

I could bike ride for at least ______miles

Now you have to remember that regular means at least a couple times a week focused on fitness, so be honest ….I enjoy the following on a regular basis: (check them off)

_______walking _______running _______jogging

_______attending a gym _______biking _______hiking

_______rock climbing _______stair climbing _______treadmill

_______weight lifting _______marshall arts _______pilates

_______working with a trainer _______elliptical _______bow-flex

_______skating _______skiing (cross country/downhill/water)

_______triathalon _______marathons

Some men have very physical jobs where they're doing a lot of working out already, construction workers etc…so, does your job give you all you need for fitness

_____yes_____ no.

80-Well now that you've had time to think about it, pick the one that suits you most:
My body is best described as:

____Adonis (Mr. Olympia has nothing on me)

____Six pack (I've really got em and not the kind ya drink)

____Toned (It may not show, but I's solid)

____Beer gut (yep I got a little bit, but its bought n paid for)

____Love handles (a little extra to hold onto on the sides)

____Big n handsome (I's a big boy, but I'm agile)

____Couch potato (Ok, I enjoy my relax time…don't worry about it)

____Average (I'm looking just fine)

____Thin (lean machine)

____Lanky (I's tall and thin)

81-We all know what we're comfortable with and some feel they have to start a routine, while others are just fine as they are. Keep heart smart they say, so what do you figure:

_____I'm just fine

_____I should do a bit more

_____I do enough already

_____I am planning to start

_____No intention of starting

_____thought about it, haven't gotten around to it

82-Habits-That's what they call things that we learn. Just seems the good habits are harder to learn and the bad ones we end up with. It could be you have a variety of them-whether smoking, drinking, swearing, fibbing, working too much. What would you say your bad one's are? (top five)

1-______________________

2-______________________

3-______________________

4-______________________

5-______________________

83-Now honesty is a big thing in life and we all appreciate it when we deal with others, but we all have ideas of what honest is, so let's just see how honest you are. Now this is when you're dealing with others and it may vary when dealing with males or females, for each, fill in the percentage of how honest you are: (use only the lines that apply and remember, they have to add up to 100%)

When talking to:	Men	Women
I tell it like it is no matter what	______%	_______%
I sugar coat at times to avoid things	______%	_______%
I do embellish, it makes things more believable	______%	_______%

I never tell a person what I really think	______%	_______%
I am only open about how I feel/think when asked	______%	_______%
I side step or avoid answering	______%	_______%
I am an open book, hold nothing back	______%	_______%
TOTAL =	100%	100%

84-Now most people say their honest, but are they really? Seems we all have different ideas on what we would consider honest.

On a scale from 1-10, you would say your honestly level is a:___________

So let's play out some scenarios and see which options you would take.

A-A woman is interested in you romantically, but you just don't feel a strong attraction. She asks you out for coffee after months of flirting with you.

____You would go out with her, because heck you're not dating anyone and she's eager.

____You would decline stating you're busy (fib?)

____You flat out tell her you're not interested even if she was the last woman on earth.

____You sit and tell her that she is just not your type as politely as possible.

____avoid the question and ask how she is to side step the whole issue

B-You find a wallet when no one is around and it has credit cards, $500.00 cash and contact information, so you:

____would contact the owner and return everything intact as you found it

____contact the owner, keep the cash and tell him that's how you found it

____take the cash, ditch the wallet someplace and no one will ever know

____turn it in to a police station just because you don't need the hassle

____call to see if a reward is offered

C-In a store, the clerk gives you change for a $50.00 when you had given a $20.00. You would:

_____point out the mistake and give them back the cash

_____say nothing and keep the extra, their loss

D-You're out with a bunch of the guys and your best friend is spewing out an incident you both witnessed. Your friend is telling a totally outrageous story that you know full well is a lie. Do you:

_____stop and correct him about the events

_____do you pull him aside and ask what the?

_____do you make light and joke to the rest of the guys about how it really happened.

_____do you say nothing, let him have his moment

E-You just had a rough day at work so your mood seems to have followed you home. You snap at someone, whether a friend, family or lover. Do you (after you calmed down)

_____tell that person what happened and apologize

_____don't bring it up again because it's over and done with

_____try to make humor and laugh about it

_____say as little as possible about it all and it will fade

Well now those were interesting scenarios, are you changing your mind about your initial honesty answer? Scale of honesty on a 1- 10 would therefore are a __________

85-We all have best friends in life and we'd do almost anything for them when they ask. So you're at home Saturday and the phone rings and it's your friend, their car died and they need help. They need you to come and get them 60 miles away, so would you go if the call came in at:

6 a.m. ______yes ______no Noon ______yes ______no

6 p.m. ______yes ______no 10 p.m. ______yes ______no

1 a.m. ______yes ______no 4 a.m. ______yes ______no

Have you ever had to do this I wonder? If so who was it for ____________________

Did they somehow compensate you for your help, if so how did they do so?

____

86-Now let's turn the tables and it's you stuck out in the middle of nowhere at 2am. So let's see about the friends in your life. How many would come and rescue you? List the names on both here, first column for yep they'd be there no matter what, and nope…not even going to call. (top 3 people)

Be there for sure anytime:	Nope they wouldn't help me out
____________________	________________________
____________________	________________________
____________________	________________________

87-Now we've all done some things that we are so grateful that we had someone looking out for us. Many times a family member or friend saved us headaches. What are friends for? They got your back and you got theirs, so who do you feel you helped out for the real important stuff and who was there for you?

They helped you	You helped them
____________________	________________________
____________________	________________________
____________________	________________________

89-Fond memories, aren't they? They are things we forget over time with life and all. It's good to reflect on important moments of the past. We're all here for a reason and some people are just meant to know each other in this life. Do you have people that you feel that way towards? Are there people you know that you just sit back and say: 'I feel like I've known you forever we were meant to meet.'

Who are they (top 6 over your lifetime):

______________________________ ______________________________

______________________________ ______________________________

______________________________ ______________________________

90-Now with all the good in our lives, we've been through some rough spots, haven't we? Those hard lessons we all go through over time. Seems we never forget the years they happened in either. We can quote it, like back in September 77 my life crapped out. What years come to mind for you? (Top 4 years)

_____________ _____________ _____________ _____________

91-Well let's get back to the sexy stuff-enough with the hard questions. If you could be intimate with anyone right now, who pops into your mind?

First: ____

Second:____

92-Do you and your friends ever compete over women? We always hear rumors about locker room talk that goes on when the buddies get together to swap stories, share moments or even to discuss issues. It could be with female friends, family or anyone. Now some have a no "kiss n tell" policy, but let's see if you've ever shared any sexual conversations:

Bragged about a conquest with friends ______yes ______no

Were you honest ______yes ______no

Talked about # of women you've been with ______yes ______no

Gone to a friend with sexual problem ______yes ______no

Lied to friends about a notch on the bedpost ______yes ______no

Talked to a woman friend to ask questions ______yes ______no

Talked to a parent to ask questions ______yes ______no

Have you ever paid for sex ______yes ______no

93-Where did you learn all you know? I mean we all start off somewhere, so how did you first learn about sex and what it can be?

______book

______porn films

______learned as you went along

______magazines

______parents

______TV shows

______from male friend

______female friend

______hired someone

______instinctual

______movies

______from a partner

94-Weird to think about, but there are many ways to learn about sex growing up. And I suppose it's good to learn all the time. There are fascinating talk shows on the TV late at night. It can be a great sexual learning tool. So let's ask if you've ever done the following to gain insight.

______read books to gain knowledge

______gone into a sex shop

______seen a professional

______watched talk shows about sex

______purchased toys for experimenting

______talked to your doctor about sex

95-Well knowledge is the key to most things in life. If there were an instruction manual on us women, life would be way easier for you men, wouldn't it? We're going to help you along here to see what you would most like to know about women. If you could ask women 5 things you've always wanted to know-Things that just confound you, whether it's how they think on one subject, why they do things a certain way or how they feel about a topic.

Think about the women in your life, no names so you're safe…what would those 5 things be?

1____

2____

3____

4____

5____

96-If you could change one thing about women in general, maybe it's the way they shop, way they talk, way they feel…what one thing would you change to make them easier to get along with?

Now let's make this tough. Pretend you had power to make this change and it lasted a lifetime and if you change that one thing, it's changed in all women worldwide forever…not just in one woman in particular.
You'd like to change:

____

____

97-Well three more questions and you are done! Whew, thought you'd never get through this, right? So for the last three we're going to focus on your life ahead.
What one thing do you want to purchase in the next 10 years

____
(could be anything)

What one person do you want to hold onto for the next 10 years

____
(could be family or friend)

What one wish do you have for your life over the next 10 years

____
(focus on just one thing)

98-You are who you are and at times we look at ourselves and want to work on something. For some they want to get ahead at work, others it's to take more time for things they love, even just wanting to learn more:

What one thing do you want to work on

____

99-You have taken the time to fill this all out, to actually put into words who you are and what you feel on a variety of things. It's a journey of laughter, memories, thoughts and wishes. If you could make any one person in your life do a book like this, just to see how they feel about things.

Who would that be _________________________________

Why____

What questions would you most want to see their answer to:

#____ #____ #____ #____ #____ #____ #____ #____ #____

100-Being single is a journey of finding who we want and what works in our life. We go through so much and we learn. At times it's hard to find exactly what we want or it seems it's what we want at the time, but doesn't work in the long run. The question is: In all your experiences, with all you've gone through with relationships, what is the one thing you have learned about yourself through it all?

____

____

Wow! 100 questions-you've done them all, aren't ya proud? I know you're probably planning ways to get back at the person who bought this for you, but isn't it good to stop for a moment and snicker at life? There are so many things that have touched your life. People, places, experiences….it made you who we are. We get too busy and never stop to think or remember moments, dreams, experiences, hopes. I believe they are important and it's what ties us together. We are all unique, but you'd be surprised at how similar we all really are. I truly hope you've enjoyed working through your hamster!

Wendy Proteau

Blessed with three siblings and parents who supported my hopes, I was raised in a small Canadian town, in an average middle-class family. Single at age forty-something, I'm still figuring life out daily. Being a combination of realist and dreamer, you can only imagine the confusion that goes on internally. Half of me writes a story with 'the happily ever after', the other half, edits the work and keeps it more realistic.

I'd never written more than a grocery list until 2009. It came out of nowhere as I sat at my computer following an idea. The '*Sit N Do Nothing Hamster Series'* is my way to bring us all a little closer in this technological world. The workbooks of self-discovery are a way to share tidbits of who we are, in the here and now. Each of the seven volumes, designed for a specific audience, asks the reader about their lives. I have many more ideas to expand the series. This hamster never quits! They are now available via print on demand.

Finding my inner voice, I decided to try my hand at a fiction. *'And When'* was written from September 2010–January 2011. Receiving many reviews, the story resonated, often bringing them to tears, laughter, and at times… needing a cold towel.

Taking months to edit the final draft, I began to miss that creative energy and '*Now What'* the sequel was started in 2012 and published in 2013. The story continues to place difficult hurdles, forcing the characters to veer from their chosen paths.

My life would be nothing without the people who have touched my soul. Friends, family, co-workers, relatives…have all been there through the good and bad. Everything takes hard work and nothing ever comes easy. Well at least not in my life. I firmly believe that karma plays an important role. It brings us the people we are meant to meet, challenges we have to overcome, lessons we need to learn and dreams we are meant to reach for.

Sit 'N' Do Nothing Hamster Series

Unlock Your Hamster-Volume One
An introduction to the series

The Single Man Hamster-Volume Two

The Single Woman Hamster-Volume Three

Hamsters Unite-The Relationship-Volume Four
Dating, Married or Living Together

Heart Broke Hamster-Volume Five
For the tough spots of break-up, divorce or loss

The Gotta Have Hamster-Volume Six
Advertising and what you buy into

The Hospital Hamster-Volume Seven
For those in hospital or home recuperating

www.ingramcontent.com/pod-product-compliance
Lightning Source LLC
Chambersburg PA
CBHW081724270326
41933CB00017B/3290
9780986898716